Original title:
Laurel Legends

Copyright © 2025 Creative Arts Management OÜ
All rights reserved.

Author: Samuel Kensington
ISBN HARDBACK: 978-1-80567-065-0
ISBN PAPERBACK: 978-1-80567-145-9

Ethereal Myths of the Forest

In a glade where shadows dance,
Squirrels hold a wild romance,
Nuts and berries fit for kings,
They twirl and leap on tiny wings.

A wise old owl with specs on tight,
Claims to read the stars at night,
But the truth is slightly clearer,
He's just after that sweet cold beer!

In the brook, a fish can sing,
He croons about the joys of spring,
Yet every tune's a little off,
He's trying hard, just needs a scoff!

The rabbits hold a grand debate,
On who should wear the crown of fate,
But as they hop and wiggle fast,
They trip and tumble—what a blast!

Guardians of the Arbor

In the forest, trees wear hats,
Squirrels dance, with acorn chats.
Woodpeckers drum, a funny beat,
While clumsy deer tread on their feet.

Raccoons hold council, under night,
Sharing tales of their goofy fright.
The owls laugh in echoes grand,
As mischief reigns in their woodland band.

Crowned with Wisdom

Old trees tell tales with rustling leaves,
Of silly critters and their heaves.
With branches high, they boast and tease,
While squirrels play tag with the breeze.

A wise old tortoise joins the fun,
Discussing nuts under the sun.
With leafy crowns, they sit and grin,
The playful bark echoes from within.

Emblems of Nature's Might

In a glade, a tall tree poses,
Claiming strength while forgetting roses.
With vines for socks, it tries to show,
How laughter makes the wild things grow.

A chipmunk jokes, "You're just a stick!"
While bunnies nod, then run real quick.
In nature's game, they share a jest,
Making mirth their humble quest.

The Forgotten Timber

Once a tree, now it's a stump,
With funny faces that like to jump.
Whispers echo in soft twilight,
As shadows dance in pure delight.

Old wood remembers wild, bright days,
As beetles march in endless plays.
Though weathered now, it stands with glee,
A goofy throne for you and me.

Graced by Nature's Touch

In a forest where squirrels wear hats,
Rabbits throw parties for chitchat chats.
Trees wear vines like a posh scarf,
While crickets serenade with a laugh.

A deer in shades does a funny twirl,
While birds above spin and whirl.
Flowers gossip in colors bright,
Nature's ball in pure delight.

Parables of the Dawning Light

Once a sunrise decided to dance,
And hosted clouds for a merry prance.
The moon was jealous, hid behind,
While stars snickered, oh so blind!

A loaf of bread flew by, so grand,
Claimed it was part of the band.
The toast joined in, all crispy and warm,
To charm the sky, a quirky form.

The Hidden Vales

In valleys where the gnomes do play,
With juggling mushrooms all day.
Dancing daisies joined the fun,
While sunflowers plotted a pun!

A goat with shades sang woeful songs,
But forgot the lyrics, went all wrongs.
The lilies laughed, oh what a scene,
In fields where silliness reigns supreme.

Heroes of the Emerald Canopy

In the canopy, the owls wore capes,
Flying around like super shapes.
The squirrels, sidekicks, gathered acorns,
This team of laughter, no time for scorns!

A wise old turtle raced up a tree,
Declaring, 'Hey, slow down, that's me!'
With the sun setting, they all took flight,
Heroes of mirth, oh what a sight!

Anointed by Growth

In a garden plump with green,
A squirrel danced, quite the scene.
With a crown of leaves, he pranced,
For the birds, he sang and chanced.

The flowers giggled at his quest,
In their petals, he'd find his nest.
A nutty king, the tales did swell,
Of the rodent who ruled so well.

Whispers of the Ancient Wood

In the woods, the trees conspire,
With whispers loud that never tire.
A raccoon listens with glee,
To tales of nuts and bold, old trees.

The owls hoot in cheeky glee,
As branches sway, they sip their tea.
Laughter echoes through each bough,
In the ancient wood, hijinks abound!

Patterns in the Bark

Bark so rough, a canvas fine,
With patterns drawn by nature's line.
A beetle claimed, 'This is my art!'
As trees sighed, 'Oh, where do we start?'

Squirrels pranced, making a scene,
Drawing patterns, quick and keen.
With acorns as their prize to remark,
They giggled at sculpting from the bark.

Beneath the Shade of the Ancients

Underneath the wise old trees,
Picnics sprout like gentle breeze.
With ants at play, and sandwiches,
The wind whispers, 'Eat and tease!'

The ghosts of woodpeckers crank,
While picnic tables surely plank.
They tell tales of what was there,
A buffet of fun, if you dare!

Unraveled in Green

In a forest so bright, a rumor awoke,
Of a tree who wore pants and a cloak.
It danced with the breeze, so carefree and spry,
While squirrels took selfies and waved as they hied.

The mushrooms would giggle, their caps held so high,
When the ivy grew tangled, they'd all start to cry.
A turtle in shades, with a can-do facade,
Claimed he'd race the wind, but he only just trod.

Stories Beneath Verdant Arches

Underneath leafy tales, so sly and discreet,
A rabbit once argued it could out-cheat.
But the tortoise, quite sly, held his ground with a grin,
While the hare napped away, dreaming of winning.

An owl told a joke that made all the foxes
Roll on the ground with their various boxes.
It's not about speed, but the laughter we share,
That makes every tale worth a sprightly flair.

Spirits of the Sagebrush

In the sagebrush wild, where the wind sings a tune,
A coyote wore boots and danced under the moon.
He jitterbugged wildly, while rabbits looked on,
Thinking, 'Who knew mornings could start with such fun?'

As tumbleweeds chuckled, they joined in the dance,
Swirling with glee in their prickly romance.
The blue jays were crooning, their feathers all bright,
Proclaiming this party, a true highlight!

Emblems of Resilience

Beneath a thick canopy, tales unfold,
Of a dandelion bold, with a heart made of gold.
While others wilted, she stood ever strong,
Singing a jig to a whimsical song.

With each tiny seed, she spread laughter and cheer,
While the daisies all giggled, their petals in fear.
A comical breeze blew, trying hard to impinge,
Yet our brave little flower didn't flinch or cringe!

Chronicles of the Gilded Branch

In a forest where squirrels plot,
They dance on branches, forgot the knot.
A twig's a throne, a leaf the crown,
Giving the acorns quite the frown.

A tree trunk whispers, tales of glee,
Of a bird who thought it could fly for free.
It flapped so hard, it took a leap,
And landed where the mosses keep.

One day a frog played king of the logs,
In a royal court of dreaming dogs.
They debated how to croak the night,
While shadows laughed at their delight.

With branches swaying, laughter grows,
Their tales fluttering like the wind that blows.
Oh, what a riot, this world unfold,
Under the sun, legends of old!

The Sway of the Majestic Bough

Beneath a bough of emerald sheen,
A raccoon wears a crown that's unseen.
He prances round, acorns in tow,
Claiming the land where the wild things grow.

A butterfly sneezed—oh what a sight!
It startled the owl and took to flight.
The branches giggled, what a parade,
As bugs joined in, a grand charade.

The mighty oak, with a crooked grin,
Offers shade where the laughter begins.
Each whisper shared among the leaves,
Keeps secrets of pranks that nobody believes.

Chasing shadows, the rabbits race,
Through a thicket of mystery, their secret place.
With every hop, their giggles resound,
In the heart of the grove, where joy's unbound!

Folklore Beneath the Canopy

Underneath the leafy cape,
A turtle tells tales of the great escape.
With a slow-motion wink and a shrug,
He spins wild stories of a snug little bug.

A fox in glasses, reading a tome,
Recites silly sonnets about making homes.
The moon chuckles, peeking to see,
What mischief unfolds so carelessly.

An acorn fell with a mighty thud,
Right on the head of a sleepy dud.
The snail, bemused, began to laugh,
At the chaos of nature that's never quite daft.

In the dance of shadows, the critters play,
Each fable grows brighter as night turns to day.
Oh, the glee that springs from roots that share,
The wonders and whimsy found everywhere!

Threads of the Verdant Myth

In the thicket where giggles often bloom,
A hedgehog narrates tales of doom.
With a needle and thread, he starts to weave,
Outlandish fables that no one believes.

The owls join in with booming hoots,
Creating a symphony from their cute suits.
They sway in rhythm, a balmy night,
While critters stumble, what a sight!

A fearless ant donned knightly gear,
Challenged a raindrop to tickle his ear.
He bowed so low, fell flat on his face,
But laughter erupted, it won the race.

Whispers of foliage drift through the air,
Entwining stories beyond compare.
In the realm where humor grows bright,
Fables flourish under the moonlight!

The Golden Laurel's Secret

In a forest bright and green,
A tree held whispers, rarely seen.
Its leaves wore crowns, oh what a sight,
They jested loudly, day and night.

A squirrel danced, a fox rolled by,
As branches chuckled, oh my, oh my!
"What's the secret?" the critters cried,
The tree just laughed, with branches wide.

The owls hooted, wise and keen,
"Search for gold where none have been!"
But glitters fade under silly skies,
While creatures play, the gold just lies.

At dusk they gather in moon's soft light,
To share tall tales of their delight.
Between the roots and leafy beds,
The laughter echoes, 'till they all head.

Shadows of the Giant's Bough

There once was a giant, tall and grand,
With a bough that stretched, like a lazy hand.
It sheltered shadows, silly and bold,
Where creatures gathered, all tales told.

A rabbit slipped on dew-kissed grass,
While a crow cawed loudly, a sassy sass.
"Is that a joke?" the bough did mock,
The hare just grinned, checking the clock.

Underneath, a dance began to sway,
As shadows beckoned, come out and play!
"Who needs the sun?" a hedgehog said,
With giggles echoing overhead.

Days passed by in giggle fits,
All thanks to that giant's silly wits.
And beneath its bough, oh what a crew,
The shadows spoke, and the world just flew.

The Spirit of the Thicket

In thickets thick, where few would roam,
A spirit danced far from home.
She laughed with leaves, a merry twist,
As critters joined, they couldn't resist.

A rabbit hopped, a porcupine spun,
While the spirit giggled, oh what fun!
"Join me here under this bush,
Where even brambles have a hush!"

The raccoons twirled, the owls did cheer,
Sipping dew drops, they had no fear.
"Who's up for riddles?" the spirit exclaimed,
And mischief thrived, never tamed.

As twilight painted shadows so fast,
They shared their secrets, a spell was cast.
In thicket's heart, where laughter thrives,
The spirit sang, and the night comes alive.

Song of the Evergreen Reign

In evergreen trees where tickles play,
A kingdom thrived in a whimsical way.
With squirrels as knights and owls their sage,
They ruled with laughter at every stage.

The pinecones bounced, like jolly balls,
As branches strummed with joyful calls.
"Sing us a tune!" cried the brave little chip,
And thus began the forest's quip.

Beneath the stars, they twirled all night,
With twinkling eyes, oh what a sight!
"Who needs a crown?" the breeze did say,
"When merriment reigns, come join the play!"

So in that forest, forever they'd sing,
Of nutty adventures and what joy could bring.
In evergreen hearts, the laughter spreads,
A melody cherished, that never ends.

Fragrance of Forgotten Heroes

In fields where heroes had a blast,
Their schemes still linger, unsurpassed.
With capes of green that flap and sway,
They pranced around in a clumsy play.

A bard once sang of silly feats,
With cheese and pies, they faced their greets.
With laughter loud, they danced away,
Each step a joke they'd often play.

Though known for might in ages past,
Their legends fade, but jokes will last.
For every sword they did not wield,
There's laughter loud in every field.

So raise a toast to all the jest,
It's humor that we love the best.
With fragrant tales and smiles to share,
The heroes laugh upon the air.

The Canopy of Dreams

Underneath the leafy shroud,
Where dreams emerge and giggles loud.
With whispers shared among the trees,
The branches sway with playful ease.

A squirrel once donned a tiny hat,
Deciding he was quite the cat,
He tried to sing, but voices croaked,
The other critters simply choked.

Beneath the moon's bright, silvery beam,
The forest bustled, not a scream.
For every dream that lost its way,
A laugh was born to save the day.

So gather near and share a jest,
For in this grove, we jest the best.
With every giggle, hope takes flight,
In dreams we find our pure delight.

Vows Under Verdant Skies

In gardens bright, two lovers vow,
With flowers dressed in laughter's glow.
They promise things that make us grin,
Like washing socks or poking kin.

The wind, it danced, a cheeky sprite,
As petals fell in silly flight.
With every laugh, a bond was made,
In quirky dreams, they waltzed and played.

Upon a throne of daisies fair,
They pledged through giggles, with no care.
"No dish will you ever need to scrub,
If I can have the last of grub!"

So lift a glass to vows sincere,
With laughter ringing, loud and clear.
For love that blooms in fun-filled days,
Is worth more than the grandest praise.

Crowned by Nature

A crown of leaves upon their head,
The woodland kings, where none dare tread.
With twigs for scepters, proud they stand,
With squirrel subjects at their command.

They sit on thrones of mossy greens,
In fantastic court of wild routines.
The jester frog leaps high and bright,
His antics make the owl take flight.

With every laugh, the kingdom grows,
For nature knows what laughter sows.
Through silly dances, colors fly,
A royal ruckus under sky.

So here's to crowns of bark and leaf,
Where laughter reigns beyond belief.
In nature's realm where fun is found,
Forever happy, kingly crowned.

Noble Crowns in the Forest

In the forest, crowns grow wide,
Squirrels dance, their tails collide,
With acorn hats, they strut about,
Chasing shadows, laughing out loud.

The rabbits wear their leafy crowns,
Playing kings and silly clowns,
While deer prance in a regal way,
Their antlers styled for a fancy day.

A wise old owl hoots from a tree,
"Respect the crown! Just let it be!"
But owls, it seems, have no sense of style,
They keep their feathers all ruffled and vile.

So, in this wood where crowns abound,
Giggles echo all around,
With nature's laughter ringing clear,
Every crown a reason to cheer!

The Heritage of Emerald Glades

In emerald glades, the tales are spun,
Of flowers that dance in rays of sun,
Bees wear helmets made of pollen,
While blossoms gossip, sweet and sullen.

The turtles rock in leafy shades,
Debating on which path to wade,
While critters scamper, quick and spry,
Chasing bugs that buzz and fly.

An ancient tree begins to snore,
As critters parade on its floor,
"It's nap time now!" the tree would say,
Yet still, they frolic, come what may.

In emerald glades, the laughter rings,
As nature plays its funny strings,
With every leaf a quirky tale,
Let's raise a cheer, let joy prevail!

Shadows of the Past

In shadows cast by ancient trees,
Wisdom whispers with the breeze,
Ghostly giggles fill the air,
As playful spirits dance and dare.

Once upon a time, they say,
Squirrels plotted in a fray,
For acorn treasures, they would scheme,
Until they tripped—a silly dream!

The old raccoon, with tales a lot,
Proclaims the forest's greatest plot,
Of hidden gems, both bright and bold,
Who knew the past could be so gold?

So in the shade where laughter grows,
Legends dance in comic prose,
With every shadow, a funny twist,
In the forest, joy can't be missed!

The Heartbeat of Flora

Every flower has a heartbeat,
Beating fast, it can't be beat,
Sunflowers sway to the rhythm,
While daisies giggle, bursting with wisdom.

The violets hum a silly tune,
Underneath the bright, round moon,
Where butterflies join in the song,
Flapping wings, they dance along.

The bulbs below sing low and deep,
As earthworms wiggle, never sleep,
In a concert of roots and soil,
The plants unite, each twist and coil.

So join the fun where laughter's found,
In every petal dancing round,
With nature's pulse in every sprout,
The heartbeat of flora brings laughs out!

Secrets of the Leafy Realm

In the kingdom where leaves do dance,
Squirrels hold a grand romance.
Nutty tales of love they share,
As acorns fly through the air.

A butterfly starts a gossip spree,
About the ants in high decree.
They claim they're building a big, tall dome,
But really, they're just lost from home.

The mushrooms throw a wild feast,
While the crickets sing at least.
A toad gives riddles, folks all stare,
As pond frogs leap through the fair.

In this realm where nature gleams,
Every plant has wild dreams.
So, if you wander here with glee,
Prepare for laughter and some spree!

Fables Wrapped in Green

Once a vine dreamed it could climb,
To touch the stars, oh what a rhyme!
But at the top, found just a bird,
Who said, 'Buddy, that's absurd!'

A branch was sure it could outlast,
The wind that blew and swayed so fast.
But every time it took a stand,
It tickled branches, wasn't planned!

The flowers gossip each day anew,
Cactus joins in, 'I'm cool too!'
They chuckle loud about the sun,
Who seems to think it's all just fun.

In this tale where greens abound,
Funny stories swirl around.
So grab a leaf, join in the spree,
Let laughter be the only decree!

The Shelter of the Wise

Underneath the wise old tree,
Rabbits gather with glee.
They share secrets of the ground,
While trying not to make a sound.

The owl rolls eyes, perched so high,
Listening to each little lie.
'That's not the way the wind blows here!'
It hoots, while chuckling in good cheer.

The raccoons dance and tip their hats,
Making fun of lazy cats.
'Stretching all day must be so tough,'
They laugh, with hearts that are quite rough.

This realm of wisdom, light and fun,
Brings together all who run.
So come if you want to play,
With wild tales to brighten your day!

Sagas of the Finely Woven

In a field where the spiders weave,
A funky band sings, just believe!
With webs as stage, they dance and spin,
Creating magic with a grin.

A grasshopper strums a tiny string,
Telling tales of springtime bling.
While beetles tap their tiny feet,
Jiving along to the beat.

The daisies sway, high and low,
As butterflies put on a show.
At twilight, fireflies join the ball,
Lighting up the garden hall.

So gather round for stories bright,
Where every creature shares delight.
In this place of woven dreams,
Life is funny, or so it seems!

The Whispering Grove

In the grove where secrets spin,
Trees gossip with a cheeky grin.
Squirrels dance with acrobats,
While owls wear their sassy hats.

Fungi joke 'bout the weather's call,
Mushrooms bicker, big and small.
Roots entwine in playful jest,
Whispering tales, a nature fest.

A deer prances, full of cheer,
Telling jokes no one can hear.
The branches sway, a laughter trail,
In every rustle, a humorous tale.

So come and visit this funny place,
Join the flora, join the race.
In the whispering grove, no sighs,
Just giggles under sunny skies!

Exaltation Among the Leaves

In a tree so tall, proud and wide,
A parrot sings with swish and slide.
The leaves dance lightly, click and twirl,
As critters plot, hats in a whirl.

A fox claims, "I'm the king of fun!"
While raccoons toast to everyone.
With acorns stacked in every nook,
They write their tales in every book.

The sunlight winks through leafy lace,
As bees competently win the race.
With laughter shared among the branches,
Nature sparkles and never blanches.

So let's all raise a glass so clear,
To joyous times, we hold so dear.
Exult in stories, wild and free,
Among the leaves, a jubilee!

The Seasons of Honor

Springtime sprouts with colors bright,
Flowers giggle in pure delight.
Summer struts in shades of gold,
While crickets tell tales, daring and bold.

Autumn comes with leaf confetti,
Squirrels argue who's the bettiest.
Winter wraps the world in white,
Snowmen chuckle, oh what a sight!

Each season brings a different theme,
Nature plays in a jovial dream.
Breezes flow with cheeky glee,
In the seasons of honor, wild and free.

Raise your glasses high and loud,
Join the frolic, be nature's crowd.
With each cycle, let's celebrate,
In this amusing dance, it's never late!

Exiles of the Forest

The rabbits plot in the moonlit night,
Whispering mischief, a curious sight.
Over the hills, they hop on a quest,
Seeking adventure, a tireless zest.

The wise old owl bumbles near,
Clueless of where he should steer.
The fox, in jest, says, "Let's get lost!"
While badgers chime in, adding to the cost.

They'll travel far beyond their home,
Wearing crowns made of twigs and foam.
As they play tag with shadows cast,
Each laugh seems to echo, sailing fast.

Exiled from boredom in the glade,
With every leap, more plans are laid.
Nature holds its breath in cheer,
For wanderers galore, the fun is here!

Chronicles Through the Foliage

In a forest deep, one tree wore a hat,
It danced in the breeze, oh what's up with that?
Squirrels held parties, oh quite the sight,
Debating the taste of mooncake at night.

The mushrooms all giggled, they tickled the dew,
While a hedgehog sipped tea, just not for the crew.
A raccoon slipped by, stealing snacks from above,
Shouting, 'Who needs a chef? I'm the one they love!'

Amidst the thick branches, birds tried out their tunes,
An owl hummed loudly, confusing the loons.
Nature's own karaoke, a symphony grand,
The critters all cheered, with a wave of their hand.

A badger told stories, while frogs croaked along,
Of tales from their youth, where they'd really gone wrong.

The trees rolled their bark, in laughter they swayed,
For life in the forest is joyfully made!

Secrets of the Verdant Legends

A fern whispered gently, 'I know a good joke!'
While the daisies blushed, behind a tall oak.
They whispered of gnomes, who danced in the rain,
And how they liked tea served with a side of champagne.

The willow, so wise, cracked a smile wide,
'The vines here, they party, they cannot abide!'
With drinks made of nectar, they flutter around,
Collecting all giggles that sparkle the ground.

A mischievous chipmunk dashed up with a grin,
'If you sprinkle some seeds, we'll all jump in!'
The toadstools all trembled and laughed till they cried,
As critters made daisy chains, side by side.

In the shade of the leaves, the grownups would sigh,
'Oh there go the kids, under brightening sky.'
They reminisced times of their own carefree days,
With chuckles and snorts, in a leafy ballet.

Tales of the Ascendant Canopy

High up in the branches, the squirrels had bets,
On which acorn would fall, oh, the silliness sets!
They rolled little dice made of twigs and old pine,
And cheered as the winds brought good luck every time.

A parrot told tales of the world far and wide,
While a snake, in the sun, slipped down for a ride.
The insects played poker, with leaves for their stakes,
While rabbits leaped high, causing humorous quakes.

The bees held a concert, buzzing sweet songs,
While flowers swayed gently, dancing along.
Ants formed a conga, to a rhythm so neat,
And laughter erupted from every small beat.

Underneath all this joy, the roots sat in glee,
They whispered among themselves, 'Just let them be free.'

For in every tall tree, and each twist in the vine,
Are stories of laughter, both silly and fine.

A Tapestry of Leaves

In a patchwork of leaves, where the seasons collide,
A dragonfly laughed, taking joy in the ride.
He twirled in the air, with grace and with flair,
While clover sprouts giggled, floating light as air.

A bear in a hat went fishing for fun,
With a frog as his friend, under warm yellow sun.
They tried flipping pancakes, which flopped in the reeds,
But cheered for the berries, the sweet tasting seeds.

Owl served old wisdom steeped in fine tea,
While insects played games, a grand jubilee.
The woodpecker drummed with a beat oh so loud,
That even shy petals swayed proud as a cloud.

The roots tangled tales of mischief and play,
Of adventures in sunlight and shadows at bay.
In this lively garden, where the laughter takes flight,
The tapestry weaves joy beneath sparkling light.

Beneath the Branching Skies

Under skies both blue and bright,
Squirrels dance in pure delight.
Chasing tails with all their might,
They throw acorns, what a sight!

A crow caws with such a flair,
Declaring that he doesn't care.
He sways from branch to branch with glee,
While chasing shadows, wild and free.

Woodpeckers drum a funky beat,
As bunnies hop, they can't be beat.
Twirling leaves in the autumn air,
Join the party, if you dare!

Beneath the trees, oh what a throng,
Silly critters sing along.
Life's a jest beneath the boughs,
Join in laughter, take a bow!

The Roots of Reverence

In the soil where secrets lie,
Worms conduct a dance nearby.
With a wiggle and a squirm,
They throw a party, all confirmed!

Grass blades gossip, soft and wise,
Telling tales of silly ties.
Roots may stretch but never fret,
They make sure their humor's set!

Rabbits munch on leafy greens,
While ants march in tiny scenes.
The daisies giggle as they bloom,
Sharing jokes in spring's perfume!

Underneath a broad oak shade,
Nature's comedy parade.
Laughing roots keep life profound,
Where all together joy is found!

Chronicles of the Evergreen Crown

In the forest, trees convene,
Whispering secrets, rarely seen.
With pinecone hats upon their heads,
They share tales of silly spreads.

The branches sway, they tell a joke,
Of a log who wished he'd croak.
But he just rolled with style and cheer,
Making all the woodland sneer.

Pine needles giggle, gleeful sounds,
Tickled by the wind that bounds.
Chirping birds bring smiles anew,
Spreading tales that tickle too!

Together in their leafy realm,
Nature's laughter at the helm.
Evergreen, they'll sing out loud,
Sharing jokes with every crowd!

Tales from a Verdant Past

Once a sapling grew so tall,
He plucked a fruit, began to sprawl.
But it slipped right from his grip,
He tumbled down, what a trip!

Mossy stones snicker, oh so wise,
As plants prepare for big surprise.
They've shaped the world with sprightly glee,
Turning history into spree.

The old tree nods with wrinkled bark,
Recalling mischief in the park.
With roots like stories intertwined,
Gnarled and funny, well-defined.

From a past where jokes still grow,
Nature's laughter steals the show.
Join the tales of verdant hue,
Where humor blooms in every view!

A Symphony of the Leaves

In the breeze, leaves twirl and spin,
Dancing squirrels join in the din.
A frog starts croaking a silly tune,
While a confused owl hoots at the moon.

A rabbit hops with rhythm so grand,
With carrots that serve as instruments, hand-in-hand.
The trees all sway, a fun-filled spree,
Nature's orchestra, wild as can be.

The crickets chirp their funny notes,
While the mushrooms giggle, wearing tiny coats.
"A symphony!" they shout in delight,
Under the sun, everything feels right.

In this green theatre of playful charm,
Every creature plays without a qualm.
It's a concert of humor, no need for a stage,
Just a patch of grass, and we engage.

Beneath the Canopy of Time

Under branches twisted and grand,
Where time's a joke, and life is unplanned.
A snail races past, or so it would seem,
While a wise old turtle lives out his dream.

A squirrel recounts tales of old,
To a crowd of mushrooms, who keep it controlled.
Laughter erupts, quite easy to find,
Beneath the canopy where thoughts unwind.

Each leaf holds secrets of moments long past,
Of pinecone parties that happened so fast.
"Come join the fun!" chirps a bright little bird,
In this leafy realm, where humor's preferred.

Time rolls like an acorn—what a funny sight!
In this wacky world, everything feels right.
So nestle under the boughs, take a seat,
Beneath the canopy, where laughter's the beat.

Shadows of the Green Realm

In the green realm, shadows dance with glee,
With playful hints of mischief, you see.
A grasshopper leaps, but takes quite a fall,
While a dogwood teases with its flowery call.

"Who's there?" asks a fern, wrinkling its face,
As shadows hide, embracing their space.
A lizard sneezes, and off it goes,
Leaving behind a trail of chuckles and prose.

The wind whispers secrets, tickling the trees,
Sending squirrels scampering, dodging the breeze.
A cheeky raccoon with a mask and a grin,
Steals your sandwich—let the fun begin!

In this green realm, don't take it all serious,
Laughter thrives, the vibes are so curious.
Shadows may stretch, but they bring out the cheer,
In the laughter of leaves, life is held dear.

The Evergreen Chronicles

In the chronicles where the evergreens grow,
Funny tales whisper, shifting to and fro.
A chipmunk declares itself king of the wood,
Draped in a leaf cape, feeling quite good.

The pinecones gossip like old ladies do,
"Did you hear 'bout the bark beetle who flew?"
Laughter erupts; it's a rollicking scene,
In a world where the wacky rules evergreen.

With roots that intertwine like a knitting club,
Even the mushrooms can't help but we rub.
A wise old oak tells the best knock-knocks,
While little acorns take silly stock.

These chronicles spin tales that never grow old,
Of critters and giggles, both brave and bold.
In the shade of green, let laughter unwind,
In this forest of fun, joy's never hard to find.

The Echo of Victors

In the field of giggles and cheer,
Where champions dance without a fear,
They flex their muscles, show their might,
But trip on roots in sudden fright.

With capes made of leaves and vines,
They strut around like silly pines,
A crown of weeds, they wear with pride,
Then fall on grass, no place to hide.

Their chants are loud, yet none can sing,
As cats and squirrels mock their bling,
Oh, the glory of those who reign,
In muddy boots, they laugh in vain.

So gather 'round, oh merry crowd,
For victors' tales are bold and loud,
In jest we toast to clumsy kings,
With laughter loud, our joy now springs.

Boughs of Honor

Beneath the branches, tales do brew,
Of heroes bold, and their odd crew,
With trophies made from twigs and dust,
They claim their fame, within we trust.

They prance beneath the leafy roof,
In capes of bark, so bold, so goof,
With jokes and jests, they rule the day,
As squirrels throw nuts in grand display.

Each branch adorned with wobbly tones,
As laughter echoes, rolling stone,
These lords of boughs, with chests so big,
Trip over roots and dance a jig.

So raise a toast to their glory ways,
With laughter bright, our spirits blaze,
Amidst the leaves where legends thrive,
Let's joke and laugh; alas, we're live!

Tales Beneath the Canopy

In the shade, where shadows play,
Legends gather to laugh away,
With faces painted green and brown,
They spin their tales, the joking crown.

Each twist of fate, a comic flair,
As branches wave, to tease the air,
A knight in branches, a jester's cap,
In forgotten tales, they plot their map.

The sun peeks through, a laughing light,
As squirrels join in this silly fight,
With berries tossed, and crowns askew,
They dance and sing a charming hue.

Beneath the boughs, great stories flow,
Of foolish acts we all know,
So gather close, let laughter ring,
In the shade, we dance and sing.

Myths in the Shade

In whispers soft, and chuckles loud,
Beneath the trees, a funny crowd,
They preach of feats, of strength and might,
Yet mischievious monsters steal the light.

With wobbly tales of flubbed designs,
And goofy stunts of wayward lines,
The heroes trip, a runaway shoe,
As laughter rolls, they all pursue.

Boots filled with mud, their shirts askew,
In quest for glory, they bid adieu,
With marshmallows thrown and vines of jest,
Their tales become the very best.

So here's to myths in sunny glades,
In jokes we find our escapades,
A legacy of laughter made,
A joyous heart in leafy shade.

Echoes of the Crowned Flame

In ancient woods where giggles roam,
A quirky beast found a leafy home.
He wore a crown made of silly twigs,
And danced with frogs like they were big swigs.

The rabbits laughed, they couldn't believe,
Their leader pranced like he had to achieve.
With every leap, they'd laugh and cheer,
As he slipped and flopped without any fear.

One day he stumbled, the crown fell down,
Landed on a squirrel wearing a frown.
With nut-filled cheeks and a snappy grin,
The forest giggled at his royal spin.

Now they tell tales at the dusk's sweet call,
Of the crowned flame who tumbled and did not fall.
In the echo of laughter, hear them say,
"Wear your crown, but keep your wits at bay!"

Legends Woven in Green

In a park where shadows love to play,
A raccoon named Fred had much to say.
He claimed he could dance like a king of the night,
But tripped on a blanket and gave quite a fright.

With a wiggle and jiggle, he took center stage,
Trying to act like a wise, ancient sage.
But instead of applause, he sparked a great chase,
As ducks joined the frenzy, adding to the race.

Fred leaped over streams with a comical skip,
His dignity lost, like a spilled bag of chips.
Legends now tell of his glorious fall,
As he bowled over turtles and set off a brawl.

Through giggles and chaos, Fred found his fame,
Not for his dance, but his wild, silly name.
So here's to the raccoon, a joy ever keen,
In the tales woven bright in a forest of green.

Emblems of the Forest's Heart

Amidst the trees stood a wise old owl,
Who wore a scarf that made folks howl.
He said, "Fashion's key to wisdom's delight,
So wear your quirks and shine through the night!"

A snail once slipped on a shiny crust,
Disguised as a hero, for fun and for trust.
He raced past the hedgehog, who chuckled in glee,
"Speed limits apply, you just have to see!"

With crickets applauding the hilarity reigns,
As butterflies giggle, ignoring the pains.
It's a fashion show in the forest's grand heart,
Where silliness blooms, and all play a part.

So if you wander where the laughter's set free,
Join in the dance of the snails and the glee.
For wisdom and fun can twirl into one,
In the emblem of joy, where antics are spun.

Requiem for a Leaf

A leaf once fell with a flip and a twist,
Claiming to know how to dance and persist.
It twirled in the breeze, with moves oh so slick,
Until it caught wind, like a clown with a trick.

The other leaves chuckled, all wrapped in the sun,
"Look at our friend, he's out having fun!"
But just as it spun, a gust came to play,
And down went that dancer in disarray.

"Farewell to the leaf!" cried a wise old toad,
"A brief shining moment, now off it's bestowed!"
Yet in the embrace of the soft forest floor,
It whispered, "New legends are what I'm made for!"

For every great tumble has a tale to spin,
In the heart of the woods, giggles always win.
So raise up a toast to the leaf in the mist,
In this dance of hilarity, nobody's missed!

Bravery Among the Canes

In fields of canes, a duck took flight,
Squawking with glee, what a silly sight!
He dared the winds, oh what a show,
Yet stumbled and tumbled, headlong to blow.

His friends all gasped, then rolled with laughter,
As he flapped back up, a true disaster!
With feathers askew and pride on the line,
He posed like a hero—what a great time!

A crow on the fence cawed jokes so loud,
Mimicking the duck, he drew quite a crowd.
"Fly high!" he cried, through fits of delight,
While our brave little duck planned his next flight.

But courage, it seems, is a funny thing,
For he leaped up high to become a king.
Only to land in a patch of dogs,
The laughter resumed—oh, what a slog!

Chronicles of Rolled Leaves

In a world of leaves, a tale unfolds,
Of the bravest snail, with a heart of gold.
He rolled his way down a slippery lane,
With visions of glory clouding his brain.

A sudden gust swept his dreams away,
He zigged and zagged, oh what a ballet!
The squirrels looked on, their eyes in disbelief,
As our snail maestro danced without grief.

Then came a beetle, stout and proud,
"Do you need a ride?" he bellowed loud.
With a shrug and a grin, the duo took flight,
Creating a whirlwind of pure delight.

Through twigs and ticks, they tumbled and spun,
As laughter erupted, oh what fun!
In the chronicles of leaves, there lies the key,
That even a snail can be wild and free!

Legacy of the Green Mantle

A frog in a pond donned a cape of green,
He leaped on the lily, a sight rarely seen.
With glimmering eyes and a ribbit of cheer,
He claimed to be king—oh, how we'd cheer!

The fishes were giggling, the turtles were shy,
As he croaked his bold plans for all to comply.
"Let's have a party, with bugs for a feast!
I'll lead the parade, from the greatest to least!"

The pond came alive with croaks and splashes,
While frogs in their capes made ludicrous dashes.
But when he slipped down with a flop and a splash,
The frogs all roared—oh, what a crash!

"Fear not," he declared, wiping off muck,
"I'll rise once again, like a fearless duck!"
With laughter and dreams, they danced through the night,

In the legacy of frogs, oh, what a sight!

Sagas of the Evergreen Wilds

In the evergreen woods, a fox told a tale,
Of the time he got lost on a wild wooden trail.
With a twist of his tail and a laugh in his eyes,
He spoke of adventures beneath endless skies.

His friends would all chuckle, their ears flopping wide,
At the thought of a fox who refused to slide.
"Why chase a mouse when you trip on a root?
Next thing you know, you're lost in pursuit!"

The owls hooted softly, the hedgehogs all grinned,
As the fox tumbled down, the fun never dimmed.
"There's glory," he said, with each tumble and spin,
"In falling face-first, my friends, you can win!"

So they danced in the moonlight, with laughter and cheer,

For the saga of the woods brought everyone near.
In tales full of mishaps, each furry friend smiled,
For mischief and laughter are always beguiled!

Legends Written in Sap

In the forest, tales unfold,
Of trees with stories left untold.
One claimed to whisper secrets grand,
While squirrels debated, 'Who's more bland?'

Sap drips slow, like time's own prank,
In thickened pools where the creatures sank.
The beavers laughed, with hats so dapper,
As the trees rolled their eyes at every clapper.

The Emblem of Nature's Nobility

Once a tree wore a crown so fine,
With acorns as jewels, it drank some brine.
The vines called it king, a glorious role,
While rabbits schemed to steal its whole soul.

A bird perched high, with a savory jest,
Claiming the crown was an unwelcome guest.
The tree just chuckled, with roots intertwined,
'What's nobility, when food's on the mind?'

Guardians Beneath the Green

Beneath the branches, shadows play,
The guardians gather at the end of day.
A raccoon jokes, 'Who's guarding who?'
While a wise old owl gives them the view.

They fumble and bumble in leaf-covered glee,
Chasing away woes, setting mischief free.
With laughter as armor, and joy in their heart,
These guardians know: fun is the best part!

Carved in the Arbor's Wisdom

Carvings and etchings tell many a tale,
Of lovers and pranksters, all set to prevail.
A squirrel once doodled a mustache so grand,
While nearby, wise trees offered a hand.

They chuckled together, both old and spry,
As the wind whispered softly, like a lullaby.
In the heart of the woods where laughter is free,
Every carving sings, 'We're all family!'

The Crowned Epiphany

Once a king wore a crown, too tight,
He sneezed, and it flew, what a sight!
Chasing it down, the entire parade,
Laughed so hard, their plans delayed.

In the court, all eyes were bright,
A jester yelled, 'Is it daytime or night?'
With crowns made of fruit, they joined the game,
And laughter echoed, who's to blame?

A hearing for fruit, they took their stand,
Banana peels tossed by clumsy hand.
The king slipped and slid, the jester took flight,
In a crown of grapes, all felt light.

So remember, dear friends, it's okay to play,
Even kings can go goofy in their own way.
In their silly crowns, they found delight,
And ruled their kingdom with sheer laughter and light.

Seeds of Time and Glory

A gardener claimed to grow seeds of gold,
But they sprouted jokes, so bold!
Merriment bloomed in every row,
Carrots with hats put on quite the show.

Tomatoes giggled as they ripened slow,
While radishes told tales of a farmer's throw.
In the field, laughter took seed,
As flowers argued over who would lead.

When the harvest came, oh what a sight,
Kale wore glasses, absolutely bright!
Spinach did pirouettes, totally keen,
In this garden of jest, they were all seen.

So plant a few smiles, let them grow,
Cultivate joy, let it flow.
With seeds of laughter in glorious time,
Every garden can be a joke-filled rhyme.

In the Glades of the Ancients

In glades where giants once roamed wide,
Tiny squirrels took up their pride.
With acorns as helmets, they marched with glee,
Pledging to conquer the tallest tree.

The owls were wise, but fell asleep,
While the squirrels held meetings, their promises deep.
Planning great feasts of nuts galore,
Forgetting their mission, they snored and snored.

One brave chipmunk led with flair,
Flipping acorns high into the air.
"Who needs giants when laughter takes hold?
In silliness, we'll find treasures untold."

So if you wander where trees touch the sky,
Remember the laughter, and don't just sigh.
The ancient tales blend with giggles and cheer,
For even the mighty must sometimes steer clear.

Boughs That Speak of Valor

In the forest, boughs whispered tales,
Of knights whose armor dragged like snails.
With swords made of twig and shields of leaf,
They battled brave spiders, beyond belief.

One knight tripped over a toadstool wide,
And declared, "To victory!" with no place to hide!
While others cheered, their laughter rang,
Echoing out as the forest sang.

Not a single dragon was ever seen,
But gossip and giggles fueled the scene.
With stick swords held high, they all took a swing,
In boughs of bravery, they learned to sing.

So gather your friends in the sun and shade,
In the woods of valor, fun will cascade.
For the tales that grow in laughter and light,
Make all the battles worth every fright.

Whispers of the Evergreen

In the woods where trees chat,
Squirrels wear hats quite fat.
The sun slips in for a peek,
Leaves giggle, dance, and squeak.

Breezes toss their leafy manes,
While critters play in lilting lanes.
Birds sing songs of silly schemes,
Dancing dreams in sunny beams.

Frogs join in, a croaking crew,
Telling tales that most won't view.
Underneath a shade so wide,
All the fun cannot be denied.

As night creeps in, the whispers play,
Nature's jesters end the day.
In this grove of giggling sights,
Joyful hearts take wondrous flights.

Crowned in Verdant Glory

Up high, the branches wear crowns,
While flowers spin in vibrant gowns.
Bees buzz with a comical whir,
A royal ball, oh how they stir!

The ants march in their tiny line,
Singing songs and looking fine.
With every step, a slip or trip,
Nature laughs at every blip.

Deer strut by, with elegance rare,
Stumbling on the fragrant air.
Squirrels watch with laughing eyes,
Chasing dreams that fill the skies.

In this realm of green delight,
Every day's a funny sight.
Crowned in hues both bright and bold,
These tales are gems worth more than gold.

Tales Beneath the Canopy

Underneath the leafy dome,
Creatures gather to find a home.
Critters swap their wittiest jokes,
While mossy floors are tickled folks.

An owl hoots with a goofy grin,
Toadstools giggle, join the din.
Woodpeckers drum a silly song,
In this forest, you can't go wrong.

Under twinkling stars so bright,
Fireflies flash with pure delight.
The ferns sway, telling tales anew,
Of mishaps shared among the crew.

In this world of green and cheer,
Laughter rings out far and near.
Beneath the leaves, let stories play,
Where every creature finds a way.

The Hushed Serenade of Leaves

The leaves rustle as if they sing,
Telling tales of the breeze's fling.
With a snicker, they brush against,
The chatter of roots so immense.

Branches sway in a dance divine,
Giggling at the sun's bright shine.
Each shadow holds a funny story,
In this grove, where woods feel hoary.

Beneath the canopy so vast,
Junebugs zoom past, having a blast.
Squirrels tease with acorn gleams,
Jumping high on silly dreams.

As twilight sets the stage for fun,
Creatures plot under the setting sun.
The serenade shall never cease,
In this heartfelt woodland peace.

The Emissary of the Woods

In the forest where squirrels chatter,
An emissary dons a hat so grand.
He speaks to trees, they laugh and flatter,
With every tale, they wave a hand.

The raccoons gather, eyes aglow,
They mimic him, it's quite a show.
Who knew the woods could be so bright,
With chortles echoing into the night?

A pinecone hat, a twig for a cane,
He wanders round like it's all a game.
But slip on a leaf, he tumbles down,
With laughter ringing, he can't wear a frown.

So if you wander, take heed my friend,
Join the laughter, let joy extend.
For the woods are alive with whimsy and song,
And the emissary knows where we all belong.

Legends in the Glimmering Shade

In glimmering shade, where shadows dance,
Legends emerge, but don't take a chance.
A talking toad croaks tales of old,
While sipping dew from leaves of gold.

Wise old owls wear glasses, it's true,
Reading stories of the morning dew.
They summon squirrels with riddles great,
While the chipmunks plot, oh what a fate!

A mischievous fox prances around,
Drops hints of treasure where it's not found.
But the legends laugh with every word,
As the forest hums, so absurd!

So stroll through the shade, yet wear a grin,
For whimsical tales always begin.
In the heart of the woods, fun-filled and bold,
Legends sprinkle laughter, pure as gold.

The Adorned Roots of Memory

Beneath the trees, where roots entwine,
Lie memories adorned, a storied line.
A gopher tells tales of his burrowing spree,
While ants march past, as spry as can be.

One day a snail took quite a long trip,
He filed a complaint on a leafy slip.
The roots, they chuckled, so wise and spry,
"It's not the pace, dear friend, but the joy of the sky!"

A raccoon pranked the hedgehog in sight,
By dressing him up in a costume quite tight.
With giggles and snorts from the crowd on display,
The roots wove legends of this grand fray.

So listen close to the whispers of old,
As the roots share laughter, and stories unfold.
In the heart of the earth, where the funny will bloom,
Adorned roots remind us there's always more room.

Grace of the Green Canopy

In the green canopy, where mischief is rife,
A squirrel juggles acorns, bringing delight.
The birds tweet secrets from high in the boughs,
While the sun sneaks in just to see how.

A chatty chipmunk with pockets so deep,
Collects loose change while the forest sleeps.
He dreams of riches beyond mere snacks,
With plans to buy cookies, if he had the knack!

Down below, the toad hops with glee,
Singing of cheese, and that's quite the spree!
Every leap creates laughter, bright and free,
As the canopy chuckles, a sight to see.

So dwell in the shade, let joy take its place,
Join the creatures in this lively race.
For the grace of the green holds a jest, you'll find,
That laughter in nature is always kind.

The Spirit of the Grove

In a grove where giggles bloom,
A squirrel donned a tiny broom.
He swept the leaves with such flair,
While rabbits danced without a care.

The trees chuckled, swaying wide,
As chipmunks played a game of hide.
Each branch whispered, "Join the spree!"
The spirit laughed, how wild and free!

A owl hooted with comic flair,
"You call this woods? It's quite a fair!"
The mushrooms bobbed with cheeky nods,
As bees buzzed by, holding their pods.

In the spirit of every thrill,
Nature played her wacky will.
With every twist and playful cheer,
The grove smiled, full of cheer!

The Triumph of the Evergreen Shield

A warrior clad in green and brown,
Stood proud in bark, never a frown.
His armor made of leaf and twig,
He danced around, oh so big!

He challenged weeds to a grand duel,
With a pinecone as his rule.
"Come at me, you bristly foes!"
With laughter ringing, off he goes!

The grasses cheered, the flowers swayed,
As he spun around, theatrically played.
"You may be bold, but I'm the best,
In this green kingdom, I'll never rest!"

In victory, he struck a pose,
The trees erupted, laughter flows.
With every giggle in the field,
The evergreen knew: he had sealed the deal!

The Mythos of Entwined Branches

In tangled branches, stories spun,
Of squirrels raising veggies—oh what fun!
They held a feast, complete with nuts,
While the hedgehogs danced, wiggly butts!

The vines intertwined with wit so sly,
Sharing tales of a pigeon who could fly.
"But he only flaps, oh what a shame!"
The roses giggled, playing the fame!

A chipmunk shouted, "Let's tell more!"
As twigs clapped hands, what a roar!
Legends told 'neath the moon so bright,
With laughter echoing into the night!

In this forest, where tales are free,
Nature's humor, as grand as could be.
So come, dear friends, let's twist and cheer,
For entwined branches bring joy most clear!

The Melodies of Nature's Crown

In a circle, critters sing,
With chirps and clucks, oh the joy they bring!
A turtle tapped, a dance to beat,
While ants marched on, to nature's heat.

The flowers swayed to the jolly tune,
Under the watchful gaze of the moon.
A caterpillar played the flute,
While butterflies spun, all in pursuit!

The rhythm bounced from tree to tree,
Filling hearts with glee, oh so free.
Every rustle, a note to play,
In this symphony of the woodsy ballet!

So let us join this merry sound,
Where fun and laughter can be found.
In nature's crown, we find our grace,
With melodies that time can't erase!

www.ingramcontent.com/pod-product-compliance
Lightning Source LLC
Chambersburg PA
CBHW071834160426
43209CB00003B/289